Increasing Profits When Buying and Selling Real Estate

Getting the most for my clients since 1992!

Acknowledgments

I love all my family and friends who helped me to finish this book. Special thanks to Alisha Renee Miller; Tony Robbins; Brian Tracy; Joel Osteen; Zig Ziglar; Larry C. Hammock, Colonel, USAF; Don S. Hendricks, SMSgt, USAF; Frederick L. Green, Colonel, USAF; Sharon R. Williams, Captain, USAF; David R. Dent, Colonel, USAF; Andrew A. Course, Lt Col, USAF; David E. Johnson, Colonel, USAF; Kenneth M. Freeman, Major, USAF; and last, but not least, Michelle Helmer Shelton.

About the Author

Author, Vaughn R. Shelton, Jr.

AKA - The Real Estate Negotiator

Nickname: Full Blast

Getting the most for my clients since 1992

FOREWORD

Vaughn Ray Shelton, Jr., began his professional career in the United States Air Force, where he was named Information Manager of the Year in 1988 and Airman of the Year for two consecutive years in 1988 and 1989. Vaughn was stationed in Loring, Maine; the Mariana Islands; and Guam, where he served as Security Police and Disaster Preparedness Specialist.

Mr. Shelton received numerous awards for commendation during his tour of duty. After graduating from the Mariana Islands University with a Bachelor of Science Degree in Business Administration, he focused his interests on the health and fitness industry until the mid-90s.

In 1998, Vaughn decided to pursue a career in real estate and became a licensed realtor in the state of Texas, where he quickly became a Top Producer with Prudential, achieving over $11 million in closed sales within one year. He earned Top Producer and Achievement Awards every year, was a member of the

Gold Medallion Club, and was selected to develop and close sales at Stone Bridge Ranch Estates located in Tomball, Texas.

Vaughn founded Certified Court Reporters and Video, LLC, a nationwide court reporting agency, in 2006. He now had a platform with which to exercise his true talents, creating and building long-lasting client relationships. Soon, Certified Court Reporters and Video, LLC was the highest-rated court reporting agency in the legal industry.

Mr. Shelton is now back where he started, at his original real estate office. Ken Brand, broker for Better Homes and Gardens Real Estate/Gary Greene Realtors, and Vaughn Ray Shelton, Jr., are now a power team once again.

In his spare time, Vaughn can usually be found burning up the hike and bike trails, strength training, and doing CrossFit. When resting from work, he enjoys watching films, reading books, or spending time with his dog Bentley and family.

TABLE OF CONTENTS

Chapter 1

Honesty and Trustworthiness

When you decide to buy or sell your next property, finding a real estate agent who is honest and trustworthy is imperative. This will help you tremendously, as having faith and confidence that your agent is working for your best interests is key to the process. From negotiations on price, terms, and conditions of the home to the sale or purchase, you will feel more confident if you trust your agent.

If you are looking to buy or sell a home, which can easily be a transaction of $200,000 or more, the integrity of the agent helping you through the process should be of paramount concern. According to the National Association of Realtors (NAR), in their 2016 Profile of Home Buyers and Sellers, 21% of home buyers and sellers listed honesty and trustworthiness as the most important factor in choosing a real estate agent. This was higher than any other factor listed for home buyers, and it was the second most important factor for home sellers.

However, depending on who you talk to and what data you are looking at, you may get very different answers regarding what the public really thinks of real estate agent integrity. That same NAR profile report suggests a high public opinion of realtor integrity, with 89% of home buyers saying they were very satisfied with the honesty and integrity of their real estate agent. Furthermore, 73% of home buyers and 70% of home sellers said that they would use their agent again or recommend them to others.

The Gallup organization, though, periodically checks to see what the public thinks of the honesty and ethics of various professions, and real estate agents have not fared well. The chart below ranks professions based upon the percentage of survey respondents who rated the profession either high or very high.

As you can see, nurses came out on top and members of Congress came in at the bottom. Real estate agents ranked in the middle, just above lawyers, governors, and business executives. Real estate agents are inserted in the graph below, using other Gallup data, as they were not originally included.

Chapter 2
Great Communication Skills

When it comes to communication, we all tend to think we're pretty much experts. The truth is, even those of us who are good communicators aren't nearly as good as we think. This overestimation of our ability to communicate is magnified when interacting with people we know well.

The researchers at the University of School of Business put this theory to the test, and what they discovered is startling. In the study, the researchers paired subjects with people they knew well and then again with people they'd never met. The researchers found that people who knew each other well understood each other no better than people who had just met! Even worse, participants frequently overestimated their ability to communicate, and this was more pronounced with people they knew well.

"Our problem in communicating with friends is that we have an illusion of insight," said study co-author Nicholas Epley. "Getting close to someone appears to create the illusion of understanding more than actual understanding." When communicating with people we know well, we make presumptions about what they understand—presumptions that we don't dare make with strangers. This tendency to overestimate how well we communicate is so prevalent that psychologists even have a name for it: closeness-communication bias.

The understanding that 'What I know is different from what you know' is essential for effective communication. Some people may indeed be on the same wavelength, but perhaps not as much as they think. They become rushed and preoccupied, and they stop taking the perspectives of others into consideration.

The strategies below will help you to overcome the communication bias that tends to hold us back with everyone we encounter, especially those we know well. Apply these strategies and watch your communication skills reach new heights.

2.1. Taking action

Communication is the real work of leadership; you simply can't become a great leader until you are a great communicator. Great communicators inspire people. They create a connection that is real, emotional, and personal. And great communicators forge this connection through an understanding of people and an ability to speak directly to their needs in a manner that they are ready and willing to hear.

2.2. Speak to groups as individuals

As a leader, you often must speak to groups of people. Whether it's a small team meeting or a company-wide gathering, you need to develop a level of intimacy in your approach that makes everyone in the room feel as if you're speaking directly to him or her. The trick is to eliminate the distraction of the crowd so that you can deliver your message just as you would if you were talking to a single person. You want to be emotionally genuine and exude the same feelings, energy, and attention that you would one-on-one. The ability to pull this off is the hallmark of great leadership communication.

2.3. Talk so people will listen

Great communicators read their audience carefully to ensure they aren't wasting their breath on a message that people aren't ready to hear. Talking so people will listen means you adjust your message on the fly to stay with your audience. Droning on to ensure you've said what you wanted to say does not have the same effect on people as engaging them in a meaningful dialogue during which there is an exchange of ideas. Resist the urge to drive your point home at all costs. When you're talking leads to people asking good questions, you know you're on the right track.

2.4. Listen so people will talk

One of the most disastrous temptations for a leader is to treat communication as a one-way street. When you communicate, you must give people ample opportunity to speak their minds. If you find that you're often having the last word in conversations, then this is likely something you need to work on.

Listening isn't just about hearing words; it's also about listening to the tone, speed, and volume of the voice. What is being said? Is anything not being said? What hidden messages exist below the surface? When someone is talking to you, stop everything else and listen fully until the other person has finished speaking. When you are on a phone call, don't type an email. When you're meeting with someone, close the door and sit near the person so you can focus and listen. Simple behaviors like these will help you stay in the moment, pick up on the cues the other person sends, and make it clear that you really hear what he or she is saying.

2.5. Connect emotionally

Maya Angelou said it best: "People will forget what you said and did, but they will never forget how you made them feel." As a leader, your communication is impotent if people don't connect with it on an emotional level. This is hard for many leaders to pull off because they feel they need to project a certain persona. Let that go. To connect with your people emotionally, you need to be transparent. Be human. Show them what drives you, what you care about, what makes you get out of bed in the morning. Express these feelings openly, and you'll forge an emotional connection with your people.

2.6. Read body language

Your authority makes it hard for people to say what's really on their minds. No matter how good a relationship you have with your subordinates, you are kidding yourself if you think they are as open with you as they are with their peers. So, you must become adept at understanding unspoken messages. The greatest wealth of information lies in people's body language. The body communicates nonstop and is an abundant source of information, so purposefully watch body language during meetings and casual conversation. Once you tune into body language, the messages will become loud and clear. Pay as much attention to what isn't said as what is said, and you'll uncover facts and opinions that people are unwilling to express directly.

2.7. Prepare your intent

A little preparation goes a long way towards saying what you want to say and ensuring a conversation achieves its intended impact. Don't prepare a speech; develop an understanding of what the focus of a conversation needs to be (in order for people to hear the message) and how you will accomplish this. Your communication will be more persuasive and on point when you prepare your intent ahead of time.

2.8. Skip the jargon

The business world is filled with jargon and metaphors, which are harmless when people can relate to them. Problem is, most leaders overuse jargon and alienate their subordinates and customers with their "business speak." Use it sparingly if you want to connect with your people. Otherwise, you'll come across as insincere.

2.9. Practice active listening

Active listening is a simple technique that ensures people feel heard, which is an essential component of good communication. To practice active listening:

- Spend more time listening than you do talking.
- Do not answer questions with questions.
- Avoid finishing other people's sentences.
- Focus more on the other person than you do on yourself.
- Focus on what people are saying right now, not on what their interests are.
- Reframe what the other person has said to make sure you understand him or her correctly ("So

you're telling me that this budget needs further consideration, right?")

- Think about what you're going to say after someone has finished speaking, not while he or she is speaking.
- Ask plenty of questions.
- Never interrupt.
- Don't take notes.

Chapter 3

Top Five Pricing Strategies for Sellers

Selling a home is not for everyone. Many people do not have the time nor the patience to deal with the process. For some, too, if the listing price is too low, the potential savings may not be worth the time and effort necessary to sell the house without a realtor. However, if you are planning to list your home, at least consider the great savings you could enjoy by selling the house on your own. If you know just a little about real estate, and you can put forward the effort to do a good job, you can save a tremendous amount of money by selling your own property.

In real estate, the "99" strategy is nearly always employed. For instance, if a seller prices their home at $599K instead of $600K, the $1K they lose will cover some of the buyer's closing costs; but in the buyer's mind, they are paying $599K. In most cases, though, knocking off $1K to bring the price below a rounded figure doesn't make that much difference to a buyer or seller. Nonetheless, there's a fair amount of psychology — and strategy — that goes into determining a home's asking price. If you're a seller, then you and your real estate agent should identify (and agree on) the approximate value of the property. Let's say you determine your home is worth around $599K, based on comparables of similar properties sold in your neighborhood and other market considerations.

The next step is to understand the price range for the list price — in this case, somewhere between $580K and $620K, depending on market conditions, competing properties, time of year, or inventory. The price range typically goes a bit higher with more expensive properties. A home worth about $1 million, for instance, could have a range from $950K to $1.05 million. Once you know your home's value and have a price range in mind, it's time to nail down the final "list" price.

3.1. Appeal to "herd mentality"

Given the high stakes of real estate, a buyer doesn't want to be the only one interested in a house. By pricing your property on the lower end of the value range, you could stimulate interest among more than one buyer and create a herd mentality. Also, if you're under the gun to sell quickly, this would be a good option.

3.2. Price it to be found in real estate searches

Most buyers tell their agent they want a three-bedroom home in a certain neighborhood under $500K (or some other dollar amount). Their real estate agent may then set up an automated buyer search in their local database for properties under $500K. But if a home is listed at $510K, that buyer will miss it. So, if your list price is higher out of the gate, you may miss a segment of buyers.

While this scenario happens frequently, many savvy agents will set up search parameters for their buyers to include properties listed a little bit more above their price ceiling. Knowing how flexible home prices can be, buyers should be made aware of properties that could be a good match for them, even if those homes are above — but within reasonable range of — what they want to pay. Often, the buyer can offer a price below the list price; or, after some time, the property will have its price reduced.

3.3. Don't get 'creative' with your asking price

Sometimes, sellers want to get creative with their asking price. I had a seller whose home was valued between $750K and $800K, and they wanted to ask $787,777. Say what? Such an oddly specific figure calls attention to itself for no good reason, like a house painted purple. Buyers will often wonder why the seller chose that figure. From there, they get curious about who the seller is, and so on.

In my experience, it's best to keep the seller far in the background, if not entirely invisible. That's why we have sellers remove all their personal belongings from their homes and decorate in neutral colors.

The goal is to showcase the property, not the seller, and to appeal to as wide an audience as possible. Getting quirky with your asking price counteracts this tried-and-true strategy.

3.4. Work out a pricing contingency plan before you put your home on the market

Oftentimes, sellers have high expectations about their property's appeal and they want to ask top dollar for it, even if their agent doesn't believe they'll get it. Or, perhaps another agent whom they have spoken to has planted a high price tag in their mind.

Whatever the reason, as a listing agent, I'll agree to try and sell the home at the higher price. But before the "For Sale" sign goes up, I always try to work out a contingency plan with the seller, just in case the property doesn't go for the desired price. By having everything on the table from the get-go, we'll have a plan B should the first plan fail. This saves time and helps set the appropriate expectations in the seller's mind so there are no unpleasant surprises down the road.

3.5. Pricing is an ongoing discussion

Ultimately, listen carefully to your agent's pricing strategy. It's their job to know what works and what doesn't. And, as with any strategy, be prepared to have an ongoing discussion about pricing with your real estate agent. Pricing a home isn't a "set-and-forget" procedure. A lot of factors can come into play when selling or buying a home, and not all of them can be anticipated. If you can be flexible and react quickly to changing market conditions or new information, you're more likely to get the best price with the least aggravation.

Chapter 4

Widen Your Network

4.1. Surround yourself with a great team

Having a team comprised of competent and trustworthy people is critical to the success of any real estate business. As a real estate developer, I am only as good as the people who surround me. In addition to professionals, with whom I work and collaborate internally, I also rely on relationships I've built with individuals and firms in my community. Establishing connections with complementary businesses – real estate industry vendors with whom you don't directly compete – is an essential networking tool. Make it your goal to identify and meet a network of vendors you can refer clients to, and vice versa. It will do wonders for your professional network.

For example, when developing a new property, I rely heavily on a master architect and contractor. An incomplete set of drawings can lead to cost overruns and construction delays. While no contractor is perfect, finding a contractor you trust is the only way to complete projects successfully. Developing a relationship with an architect who is familiar with local zoning codes is essential, too. Whether an architect and contractor work well together can make or break a project. If they do not work cohesively, construction delays can result and will inevitably eat into your planned operating income.

Similarly, if your client is unfamiliar with the mortgage lending process, direct your client to a trustworthy lender who can help navigate what is often a stressful and important financial decision. By maintaining good banking relationships, developers can improve your chances of engaging in a successful transaction.

4.2. Create a professional website and blog

Treat your real estate business as if it were a digital media business and go paperless as often as possible.

In regard to visual appeal, my own personal belief is that every house tells a story – all too often, however, the character and story of a home are lost in its listing description. In the spirit of keeping readers well-informed, a good blog needs to publish new, original content on a regular basis. Increasingly, a person's first impression of a home doesn't form at the front door but, rather, on the computer screen before the showing. Make use of local imagery; don't rely on stock building and property photos. In many ways, you're not just selling a house; you're selling an entire geographic culture. Showcase the best that your area has to offer by publishing high-resolution photos of local town landmarks and familiar sites. Successful real estate is often the product of great photography.

It also helps to be an expert and a scholar of your industry. Know what real estate apps people are using and stay updated on new developments, innovations, and trends in the field. What real estate blogs do your clients read? What hashtags are being used at the conferences you attend?

4.3. Social media

Social media has become a powerful tool for connecting with your clients; it also creates great opportunities to share your knowledge and expertise with them in an easily accessible format. When using social media, respond to all inquiries, emails, and messages across all channels swiftly. Interact with users, share good press, and promote your properties. Make yourself easy to contact and be an active user on multiple channels. Use Facebook and Twitter to share your listings and promote your properties on major real estate aggregators like Zillow and Trulia. Be sure to keep your voice authentic—you want to avoid coming across as though you are desperate to sell something.

4.4. Attend conferences and industry events

Remember that real estate networking events are about engaging with other professionals in your industry. Treat conferences as opportunities to learn about all the new market information and innovations your colleagues are using. Share conference thoughts in realtime on social media. Don't just network within your industry – diversify. If you have been living and working in your area for a long time, you might already be buddies with the other realtors in your area. Try to expand your geographical network by engaging with influencers from other regions. These new connections can offer new ideas and strategies. Also, make it a point to look up your past connections for coffee or drinks. This is a great way to both maintain and strengthen your relationships.

4.5. Engage in your local community

Knowing how to build rapport with others and relate to different types of people is key when it comes to networking. For real estate developers, establishing a consistent presence within your own community is important, too. I can't overemphasize the importance of being an active participant in your community. Community involvement will not only expand your client base, it will strengthen your knowledge of the neighborhoods where your properties are located and of the people who live in them. Real estate professionals can develop their community presence in a myriad of ways.

4.6. Local sponsorship

Sponsor local festivals, little league teams, or school events. Signing up as a community sponsor often results in securing a logo spot on T-shirts, program pamphlets, or flyers. This is great for branding and business recognition.

Spend several hours each month donating your time to local groups and organizations. If you want to keep within the real estate theme, volunteer for a local chapter of Habitat for Humanity, or reach out to an affordable housing advocacy group in your city. This is an excellent way to both expand your network and have a positive impact on your community.

Reach out to your local radio station. Public radio shows always need content. It's likely that you can help them out by lending your voice to a show or podcast segment.

Consider collaborating with local schools during career days; it's an engaging way to generate real estate leads. Further, if any local colleges or universities offer real estate courses, reach out to them, and offer your expertise. If your business is open to the idea, propose starting an internship program with a local college.

Finally, join local networking groups, nonprofit boards, or arts associations whose activities interest and inspire you.

Chapter 5

Negotiation Skills

Negotiation is a method by which people settle differences. It is a process through which compromise or agreement is reached while avoiding argument and dispute. The following are the top eight negotiation skills you should master.

5.1. Preparation

Before entering a bargaining meeting, the skilled negotiator prepares. Preparation includes determining goals, deciding on areas of compromise, and planning alternatives to the stated goals.

5.2. Active listening

Active listening involves the ability to read body language as well as verbal communication. It is important to listen to a realtor to find areas for compromise during the meeting. Instead of spending the bulk of the time in negotiation expounding the virtues of his viewpoint, the skilled negotiator will spend more time listening to others.

5.3. Emotional control

It is vital that a negotiator possess the ability to keep his emotions in check during the negotiation. While a negotiation on contentious issues can be frustrating, allowing emotions to take control during a meeting with a realtor can lead to unfavorable results.

5.4. Verbal communication

Sellers must have the ability to communicate clearly and effectively to the other side during the negotiation. Misunderstandings can occur if the negotiator does not state his case clearly. During a bargaining meeting, an effective negotiator must have the skills to state his desired outcome as well as his reasoning.

5.5. Problem solving

Individuals with negotiation skills have the ability to seek a variety of solutions to problems. Instead of focusing on his ultimate goal for the negotiation, the adept individual can focus on solving the problem, which may be a breakdown in communication, to benefit both sides of the issue.

5.6. Decision-making ability

Leaders with negotiation skills possess the ability to act decisively during a negotiation. This may be necessary during a meeting with a realtor to agree to a compromise quickly and end a stalemate.

5.7. Interpersonal skills

Effective negotiators have the interpersonal skills to maintain a good working relationship with a real estate agent. Sellers with patience and the ability to persuade a realtor without using manipulation can maintain a positive atmosphere through a difficult negotiation.

5.8. Ethics and reliability

Ethical standards and reliability in an effective negotiator promote a trusting environment for negotiations. Both sides in a negotiation must trust that the other party will follow through on promises and agreements.

Chapter 6

Scope of Good Humor

For a real estate agent, it is beneficial to maintain good humor with clients, because this allows the agent to facilitate a trusting relationship.

A few weeks ago, I was feeling frustrated with the daily routine, so I texted two of my closest friends. "Rough day," I quickly tapped out in a message. "I need something to cheer me up."

My inbox was soon filled with uproarious statements, GIFs, and all-around monkey business. After some time, I was relaxed and light-hearted, especially as compared to what I had been feeling throughout the day. My friends possess the ability to make me laugh. Chances are, I'm not alone in this. We all have that one person in our lives who, no matter the circumstances, can put a smile on our otherwise scrunched faces. Research says that everyone has the ability to comprehend humor within the first phases of life. But while we all may have the potential for this funny bone, it takes a special kind of person to make an entire group erupt with amusement.

As the old saying goes, "Life's better when you're laughing"; and no one knows that better than friends who share a sense of humor. When these groups prioritize laughter, they're happier and healthier for it.

Research has shown that smiling works as a mood booster, while laughing releases tension and stress. I practice self-acceptance, which is also important. We can't all be as funny as Jennifer Lawrence (although we might wish to be); a person who is open to their faults and who publicly makes fun of their pitfalls is often the funniest, but even people with a light-hearted attitude who practice more self-acceptance than most are appreciated. Good-humored individuals accept their flaws and laugh them off in a healthy way. This is something we all should work towards.

While humor is indeed a key to a happier life, it's not necessarily suitable for all situations. My team and I are very meticulous. There's a line between well-intentioned humor and mean-spirited jokes, and those with good humor know the difference. "Most comedy is based on getting a laugh at somebody else's expense. I find that that's just a form of bullying in a major way," comedian Ellen DeGeneres told CBS News in 2012. "So, I want to be an example that you can be funny and be kind and make people laugh without hurting somebody else's feelings." Humor, in this way, can give people physical comfort. Laughter, in fact, is the best medicine, and people who have a good sense of humor use this to their advantage. Those giggles can clear up the blues, recover your immune system, and even alleviate pain.

Overall, humor can help us both physically and psychologically. An associate professor who studies emotions, Peter McGraw, PhD, at the University of Colorado, Boulder, writes for *Psychology Today*,

"When done well, humor can have a significant positive effect on your life. By developing a better understanding of humor, we believe we can then suggest ways that people can live better lives—from helping them cope with pain and stress to encouraging people to use humor to criticize brands that have done them wrong."

While most people fret with each annoyance, each passing birthday, and each unexpected turn, good-humored individuals take it all in stride. A study shows that wittiness, in fact, increases resilience well into retirement. All of this, and the above-mentioned points, show that humor is a very useful tool for both the seller and the realtor to ensure a positive collaboration.

Chapter 7

Top Questions to Ask When Selecting a Real Estate Agent

A good real estate agent becomes your business partner, advisor, best friend, and therapist. Choose wisely, or you'll be stuck with someone you don't see eye-to-eye with—or worse, someone you don't trust. "Don't work with somebody because they say they'll cut their commission," says Bonnie Fleishman, the #3 real estate agent in Glen Burnie, Maryland. "Use somebody you feel confident is going to give you the best advice."

In 1998, sold homes were on the market a median of four weeks, but sellers' time with a listing agent can extend even two months longer, says Fleishman. Before a home goes on the market, a good real estate agent will recommend the necessary design changes, remodeling, and staging. You will likely speak with your agent every day; and when offers start to come in, you'll speak with your agent several times a day. That's why you need an all-around amazing real estate agent who you know you'll get along with well.

Interview several agents before deciding upon one—if they can't answer some of these questions to your liking, find someone else. When doing background research, you'll find the answers to a lot of the most important questions on an agent's Home Light profile. For a great example of a helpful, data-fueled agent profile, check out San Francisco's Ron Abta.

Do not settle until all the answers are to yours and your family's satisfaction. So, what are the important questions you should be asking?

7.1. May I see your real estate license?

No-brainer, right? Always ensure you're working with a trained, accredited professional. Every listing agent should be prepared to deliver proof of their license to sell in your area. If they can't deliver, move on, because something shady is going on.

7.2. Will you pass along a list of referrals?

Like a license, every listing agent—and home buyer's agent for that matter—should arrive at a first meeting with referrals. If they do not, ask for them. Be wary if an agent can't offer a handful of client names to call.

7.3. What are your listings' average days on the market?

Always ask to see how long their listings sit on the market. Compare this number to other agents interviewed; and if theirs is oddly high, ask for an explanation. If they can't attest to why, then find another agent.

7.4. What is your list-to-price ratio?

An agent can show the prices at which they list a home, but more important is to see how that compares to the price at which the homes actually sell—up to date, of course. A good list-to-price ratio will depend on the market and location, but be wary of percentages too far below 90%. Also, if an agent's ratio is skyrocketing over 100%, be careful of their strategy. They could be underpricing homes to pad their ratio. You should also request specific details about their motivation for the listing prices they offer.

7.5. Have you sold homes in this neighborhood?

Communities differ greatly in terms of the types of homes that sell, what buyers in the area want, and more. Plus, to sell a home, agents are also selling the neighborhood and its perks. If an agent has experience in your specific neighborhood, it's a major advantage.

7.6. Have you sold homes in this price range?

Price range can dramatically alter decisions for the marketing and selling of a house. Agents should understand the market, period.

7.7. How long have you been a real estate agent?

Be cautious of new agents, but this shouldn't be a deal-breaker if they have stellar referrals.

7.8. Are you a part-time or full-time agent?

Be far more cautious if an agent is part-time. Selling your home needs to be a full-time job, and they should be focused solely on achieving that goal.

7.9. How many sellers are you currently representing?

Focus is a concern for agents who are juggling several listings. You don't want to get lost in the shuffle.

7.10. What is the ratio between buyers and sellers you represent?

Listing agents need to be experienced in, of course, listing. If history shows far more experience on the buying side than the selling, don't let it be a deal-breaker, but make sure you're comfortable with the agent's answers to all the other questions. You could benefit from having a network of eager buyers at your disposal.

7.11. Will I be working with you directly or with a team?

There is nothing more frustrating than getting comfortable with an agent and then seeing someone new at every meeting. A small team is OK—it means more resources and assistance—but get introduced to everyone. Don't allow your home to be another nameless, faceless listing.

7.12. How do you plan to market the home?

Every realtor should enter this partnership with a plan—period.

7.13. Do you have "X, Y, Z" in your network?

Experienced listing agents should, at a minimum, be able to recommend the following: a lawyer specializing in real estate, mortgage advisor, handyman, home stager, house cleaner, a locksmith, and moving company. Part of the benefit of working with a real estate agent is access to their vast network.

7.14. How do the realtor fees work?

There should be no surprises – try to understand ahead of time how to pay the realtor. Typically, listing agents work under a split commission. This also applies on the buyer's agent's side. When the seller pays a listing agent, the 6% commission is typically split four ways. Two brokers and two agents split the commission on nearly all real estate transactions.

7.15. Will you explain the home selling process from start to finish?

Ask your agent to briefly describe all the processes involved in a sale. Everything should be obvious so you have a clear sketch of the selling procedure to avoid any ambiguity.

7.16. What is the best way to contact you?

A realtor should never be out of touch, within reason.

7.17. May I see a written comparative market analysis?

A CMA is step one of determining a price for the house. It examines the neighborhood, showing prices at which similar properties are sold. If you want to see an in-depth view of how one of these comparative market analyses is done, we found a pretty good run-down on Fit Small Business.

7.18. What is the price range for this home?

Always acquire from the agent the market price range for your home.

7.19. What do you think will be the selling price for this home?

My team and I believe that this is the second most important question to ask a realtor. When it's a trusted realtor, they should give you a reasonable answer with reasonable advice to get there, even if it may be hard to hear—i.e. a remodel, removing all family photos, a new roof, painting over a beloved mural, etc.

7.20. How can we best work together to sell this house?

The agent-seller relationship is a partnership. Ask what you can do to help.

7.21. What can I do to get this house ready for showings?

Selling a home can sometimes be a full-time job for sellers, too, to keep a house spic and span for home showings, for instance. "The team and I remind our sellers they have to get up early, they have to make their beds and put the dishes in the dishwasher," Fleishman says. "If they want to get top dollar for their house, they have to be in top condition."

7.22. Do I need professional stagers for my home?

A professional and experienced real estate agent will come up with a plan for showings regarding how the house should look. That could include professional stagers—which a good agent will provide for free.

7.23. What should I already be packing up?

Preparing for a listing and then showing the home will almost always include the sellers removing personal property from the home, whether a professional stager is involved or not. Ask what the realtor believes should go—the clutter of children's toys, the wall full of family photographs, the bed from a room that will be staged as an office—and get a head start on packing for the move.

7.24. What are the closing costs for a buyer?

Be prepared for the upfront costs that sellers may need when closing on a home offer. The total costs will depend on the buyer's offer, but an agent should be able to estimate the money a seller will need on hand. This can include attorney fees, title fees, broker commission, appraisal fees, and more. The example shown on the next page is developed based on a $250,000 property and using a conventional loan.

Loan Origination Fee $2,500 (1%), Discount Fee $625 (0.25%), Processing Fee $450, Underwriting Fee $500, Wire Transfer $25-$50, Credit Report $35, Tax Service $50, Flood Certification $20, Title Insurance $550, Escrow/Signing $450, Courier Fee $20, Appraisal $450, Recording $110, Homeowner's Insurance First Year Premium $700, 6 Months' Property Tax Reserves $1,500

Chapter 8

Increase Your Home Value

Now it's time to roll up your sleeves and get to work! Selling a home, after all, entails a whole lot more than just planting a "For Sale" sign on your front lawn or uploading a few random photos of your place— especially if you're angling for the most cash. You need to do some due diligence and prep work in getting your home ready for sale.

So, before you put your house on the market, peruse this checklist of things you must do in preparation. Some of these tips are surprisingly easy, while others might require a little bit more time and elbow grease.

In any case, they're bound to pay off once buyers start oohing and ahhing over your place—and hopefully ponying up a great offer.

8.1. Find the real estate agent

Finding the right real estate agent should be your first step. If you aren't selling the home by yourself, you'll need to do your research and follow some of the advice I've given you so far in this book.

8.2. Curb appeal

Make sure the first thing prospective buyers see of your home entices them to want to see more. Yes, for better or worse, buyers do tend to judge a book by its cover. By investing some effort in relatively easy fixes, like planting colorful flowers and repainting your front door, the outside of your house can beckon them in and make them more likely to buy.

8.3. Declutter - home, garage, closets, and attic

Less is definitely more when it comes to getting your house ready to show. Do a clean sweep of counters, windowsills, tables, and all other visible areas, and then tackle behind closed doors—closets, drawers, and cupboards—since virtually nothing is off limits for curious buyers. If the house is overflowing with stuff, they might worry that the house won't have ample space for their own belongings. Take the excess and donate it or pack it up into storage. The bonus to taking care of this now is that it's one less chore you'll have to do when it's actually time to move.

8.4. Depersonalize your space

The next step on your declutter list? You want to remove any distractions so that the buyers can visualize themselves and their family living on the property. This includes personal items and family photos, as well as bold artwork and furniture that might make your home less appealing to the general public. The goal is to create a blank canvas on which house hunters can project their own visions of living there and loving it.

8.5. Repaint walls to neutral tones

You might love that orange accent wall; but if it's your potential buyer's least favorite color, that could be a turnoff. You are safest using a neutral color, because it's rare that someone will hate it; but the other benefit is that a light, neutral color allows buyers to envision what the walls would look like with the color of their choice.

8.6. Touch up any scuff marks

Even if you're not doing a full-on repainting project, pay special attention to scrubbing and then touching up baseboards, walls, and doors to make the house sparkle and look cared-for.

8.7. Fix any loose handles

A small thing, sure, but you'd be surprised by the negative effect a loose handle or missing light bulb can have on a buyer. It can make them stop and think, "What else is broken here?"

8.8. Add some plants

Green is good because plants create a more welcoming environment. You may also want to consider a bouquet of flowers or a bowl of fruit on the kitchen counter or dining table.

8.9. Conduct a smell test

Foul odors, even slight ones, can be a deal breaker, and the problem is that you might not even notice them. The team and I recommend inviting an unbiased third party in to try to detect any pet smells or lingering odors from your kitchen. If the smells are pervasive, you might need to do some deep cleaning, because many buyers are on to your "masking techniques" such as candles or plug-in room deodorizers.

8.10. Clean, clean, clean

And then clean some more. You want your property to look spotless. Take special care with the bathroom, making sure the tile, counters, shower, and floors shine.

8.11. Hide valuables

From art to jewelry, make sure that your treasures are out of sight, either locked up or stored offsite.

8.12. Consider staging

Does your house scream 1985? Nothing invigorates a house like some new furnishings or even just a perfectly chosen mirror. The key is getting your home staged by a professional. Home stagers will evaluate the current condition of and belongings in your house and determine which elements may just raise the bar. They might recommend that you buy or rent some items, or they might just reorganize your existing furniture in a whole new way.

Chapter 9

Getting Ready to Sell Your House?

According to a recent report from *Remodeling* magazine, curb appeal projects, such as changes to windows, siding, and doors, lead to a higher return on investment than interior improvements.

Over the past 30 years, *Remodeling* has compared the average cost of improvement projects with their value at resale, based on the experience of real estate professionals. In the 2017 Cost vs. Value Report, there is support for the generally held opinion that today's home buyers, while still enthusiastic about the bells and whistles, want to ensure their homes are structurally sound with all systems functioning efficiently.

Remodeling tracked projects including a basement remodel, an entry door that was replaced with 20-

gauge steel, and the addition of stone veneer, among others. The average return among all 29 projects was 64.3 cents per dollar spent.

Among the trends was the higher return of curb appeal projects and projects that required the replacing of windows, doors, etc. Replacement projects generally scored higher than remodeling projects; the ROI of replacement was 74% and of remodels was 63.7%.

As in the previous year, adding loose fill insulation to the attic returned 107.7% and was the only project on the list whose value exceeded its cost. Steel door replacement and addition of stone veneer also paid off, at 90.7% and 89.4%, respectively. Interestingly, these are among the cheapest projects, although their costs were up over the previous year.

Those who want to tackle an interior project could do well to consider a basement remodel. Providing it's done well, a high-end basement remodel was perceived as high-value, returning 7.4% more than the same project last year, while a mid-range basement remodeling project only increased in value by 3.3% over the previous year.

Chapter 10

Are You Really Saving Money?

One of the most common reasons for someone to try to sell a house without a realtor is to save money by avoiding a commission fee.

"This is a very valid reason," says Deb Agliano of Re/Max Andrew Realty in Medford, Massachusetts. "The problem is, buyers know the seller isn't paying a commission, so they take that into consideration and make a lower offer."

Like any other real estate transaction, the final sale price, who pays for any commission, home warranty, and closing costs are all negotiable. Sellers without an agent need to be savvy in order to come out on top. According to the National Association of Realtors, in 2014, the average For Sale by Owner home sold for

$210,000, versus $249,000 for a home sold by a real estate agent.

"In most cases, people think they won't pay any commission at all," says Jason Bowman of The Jason Bowman Team at Re/Max Elite in Mason, Ohio. "But if the buyer has an agent, you'll have to pay their 3 percent commission. And the fundamental problem is, the buyer's agent represents the best interests of the buyer only—and you wouldn't know the difference because you're not entrenched in the business every day."

In the hunt for a new house, K. Lee Tomlinson, Jr., of Peyton, Colorado, wanted to buy an FSBO property. He says he's thankful his real estate agent, Ami Quass, was willing to tackle the extra paperwork produced by a seller who was unsure of the process.

"The realtor ends up having to represent both parties, once both parties agree to start working a deal," he says. "Which means the realtor ends up having to be not only the buyer's realtor, but also has to accomplish work that normally a seller's realtor would do. The seller agreed to pay commission."

Consider a house with a sloping front yard. Selling a home yourself requires meticulous attention to detail in order to obtain the optimum price and avoid litigation after the sale.

Do you really have the time? It's after dinner—you're curled up on the couch watching TV and there's a knock at the door from a potential buyer (or maybe just a nosy neighbor). Is it safe? Is it legitimate? How would you know?

"Does a potential seller really want to answer calls or a knock on their front door from complete strangers and invite them into their home for a look?" asks realtor Deborah Colman in Folsom, California. "An experienced agent will meet with and pre-screen a potential buyer prior to showing homes. The agent will also ensure that the buyer is pre-approved for the price range in which they're looking."

Safety and privacy are also points to consider when selling a house without a real estate agent. "Realtors have sophisticated tracking devices when monitoring your home during a sale process," says Jonathan D. Reed of Fairfax Realty in Fairfax, Virginia, noting that any agent showing a home must seek permission, schedule an appointment, and obtain a unique security code to access the house. "A realtor can screen visitors to your home and follow-up with clients who have toured it."

Do you pay attention to details? "The list of potential mistakes is huge," says Realtor Erick Monzo of Keller Williams—The Monzo Group in St. Clair Shores, Michigan—"unless you know how to read closing documents, fill out purchase agreements, and calculate the true value of a property. Every state has different laws and regulations regarding real estate transactions. I believe the scariest mistake by not crossing your T's and dotting your I's is you leave yourself open to future litigation."

The biggest mistake that For Sale by Owners make is to underestimate the complexity involved during the entire process. I have heard several stories about deals falling apart after the buyer and seller have agreed on the terms because financing collapses. One of the realtor's duties is to pay attention to the details at every step of the way.

The general public isn't aware of everything involved in getting a home ready to sell. They don't see all that's involved in shepherding a transaction to a successful conclusion, including the many deadlines, dozens of mandatory documents, or hundreds of emails and phone calls. It's a full-time job.

Top 10 Reasons Why FSBO Owners Do Not Sell Their Real Estate Property

- Sellers do not know how to prepare the home correctly before listing for sale.
- Sellers do not know how to screen potential buyers.
- Sellers are not available to handle property inquiries.
- Sellers do not allow potential buyers to view the home without pressure.
- Sellers do not know how to negotiate with potential buyers' offers/contracts.
- Sellers do not know how to handle the home inspection findings.
- Sellers are not willing to (or are unable to) pay a commission to a buyer's agent.
- Seller's home is lacking marketing exposure.
- Sellers did not price their home correctly.
- Sellers do not know how to ensure the deal will be brought to a close.

Chapter 11

Why Choose Vaughn R. Shelton?

11.1. My team and I promise to tell you the truth about your property. I will give you my honest assessment of what your home is worth. I won't mislead you about its value just to get your listing or make you feel good.

11.2. My team and I promise to disclose all my relationships in the transaction. If I am representing both the buyer and the seller in our transaction, I am obligated to tell you. However, there are other kinds of relationships that may influence our business together; so if you're thinking of buying my brother-in-law's house, I'll tell you that, too.

11.3. My team and I promise not to put my commission ahead of what's best for you. Of course, I earn more money if you buy a $400,000 house instead of a $300,000 house. But if the $300,000 house is clearly best for you, I will respect your choice and work hard to complete the deal successfully all the same.

11.4. My team and I promise to respect your confidences. Over the course of our working together, you may share personal, financial, and other confidential information with me. I will not disclose this information to anyone, nor will I use it to gain any kind of advantage in a transaction.

11.5. My team and I promise to show you all the available properties in your price range. Some realtors may try to steer you toward their own or their company's listings.

11.6. My team or I will show you any property that meets your needs, regardless of who has the listing.

11.7. My team and I promise to give you good advice. I deal with lenders, home inspectors, appraisers, and countless other professionals on a regular basis. I can give you solid recommendations about these matters should you need them; and if I think you might be making a bad choice, I'll tell you.

11.8. My team and I promise not to push you into a bidding war. Real estate is a competitive business, and there are offers and counteroffers that take place during any business deal. However, I will not encourage you to go beyond your maximum budget to buy a property. I won't tell you that other people are interested in the property or are about to make offers in a bid to get you to make a higher offer.

11.9. My team and I promise that you will understand what you're signing. Any real estate deal involves a mountain of paperwork. You'll be asked to sign all kinds of documents, and I will explain them all to make sure you are comfortable every step of the way. I won't get you into a time crunch so that you feel you don't have time to thoroughly read the paperwork.

11.10. My team and I promise to tell you the truth about myself. I'll provide you with information about my background, my training, and my experience as a realtor. I won't make any false claims. I'll discuss my commissions and any other compensation I might receive as a result of our transaction.

11.11. My team and I promise to follow through and follow up. I don't list and leave. I'll discuss with you exactly how I work and what you can expect. I'll communicate regularly, and you'll know everything that's going on as soon as I know it. Even after we close the deal, I'll keep in touch to be sure you're still happy with the way things turned out.

11.12. Sellers will receive a detailed overall report on showing activity and feedback. My team works very hard to ensure that we make several attempts at receiving feedback from our showings. Persistence is key!

11.13. Sellers will receive weekly reports on marketing, advertising, and showings.

11.14. Sellers have my team of account representatives — who will be doing marketing, prospecting, cold-calling, and following up on every single call and lead regarding your property — at their disposal.

11.15. Sellers receive weekly efforts in the form of feedback from brokers, agents, and internet traffic on your real estate property.

11.16. Sellers receive an MLS Listing Sold report monthly.

11.17. Sellers will receive an Active Listing report showing foot and web traffic for their listings.

11.18. Sellers will receive a list of lease listings.

11.19. Sellers will receive a list of pending listings for their property.

11.20. Sellers receive a marketing report across all areas from social media that includes website traffic, calls made, showings, and feedback.

11.21. Sellers also receive a monthly press release regarding property listings they have listed for sale.

11.22. Seller's property will be listed for sale on the below websites:

Homefinder.com, Realtor.com, Ebay.com, MLS.com, Zillow.com, Trulia.com, Facebook.com, Amazon.com, Homes.com, Redfin.com, Craigslist.com, Fizber.com, Oodle.com, FindMyRoof.com, WebClassifieds.com, PressRelease.com, and MyHome.com

There are also many more websites where your property will be listed. Ask for a complete list for your review!

11.23. National and international advertising with https://www.realtor.com/international/ and https://www.listglobally.com will be implemented to ensure the sale of your house.

Chapter 12

Vaughn's Expertise and Background

12.1. Experience - 35 years' experience in all areas of real estate -- sales, marketing, and details of the real estate transaction (1992 – present).

- Closed up to $15 million in production and sales in one year.
- Rated top 5% in real estate for new listings and solid marketing and customer service.
- Specializing in the areas of Tomball, Champions/1960, Lake Conroe, and The Woodlands.
- Expired listing expert and specialist since 1998. Selling homes other realtors can't.
- FSBO listing expert and specialist since 1998.

12.2. Military awards

- United States Air Force Administrator of the Quarter - April - June 1998

- United States Air Force Outstanding Information Manager of the Quarter - April - June 1989
- United States Air Force Outstanding Airman of the Year in 1989 and 1990
- United States Air Force Information Manager of the Year in 1990
- United States Air Force Outstanding Achievement Award - 1990
- United States Air Force Outstanding Service Award - 1990 and 1991
- United States Air Force Superior Service Award - 1992

12.3. Achievement awards

- Mary Dillon Custom Homes - Rookie of the Year - 1995 and 1996
- John Parks Custom Homes - 1997 - 2000
- Keller Williams - Excellence Award - 1997
- House Hunters - Top Producer - 1998
- House Hunters - Top Sales - 1998

- House Hunters - New Home Sales Award - 1998

- Stonebridge Ranch Estates - Outstanding Customer Service Award - 1998

- Stonebridge Ranch Estates - New Home Sales Award - 1998

- Prudential New Home Sales Award - since 1999

- Prudential Real Estate Gold Medallion Club - since 1998

- Prudential Real Estate Excellence Award - since 1998

- Prudential Real Estate Top Listing agent and Top Sales Agent - since 1998

- Gary Greene and Better Homes and Garden - Community Service Award - 1999-2005

12.4. Education

- (BS) Major in Management and Business. Guam University (GU) - 1988-1990

- (MA) Minor in marketing and advertising. Guam University (GU) - 1987-1998

- Management, Communications, and Leadership. United States Air Force Academy (USAF) - 1987-1994

- Real Estate Brokerage - Champion Real Estate Academy of Massachusetts - Real Estate Brokerage and Agent Training - 1990 and 1991

- Texas Central College (TCC) - 1995 to Present

- Tomball College (TC) - 1995 to Present

- Champions School of Real Estate (CSRE) - 15 courses relating to all areas of real estate - 1996

- Prudential Real Estate Professional Real Estate Career Training - since 1998

- Houston Association of Realtors (HAR) – E-Certification Designation - 2000

- Houston Association of Realtors (HAR) - New Home Pro Training - 2002

- Champions School of Real Estate (CSRE) - Marketing, contracts, communications, law of agency, real estate inspection, finance, and appraisal – 2017-2018

12.5. Professional training

- United States Air Force (USAF) - Disaster Preparedness Leadership School - 1988
- United States Air Force (USAF) - Information Security Program - 1988
- United States Air Force (USAF) - Disaster Preparedness Training - 1987-1994
- United States Air Force (USAF) - OJT Trainer/Supervisor on Chemical Warfare Training - 1989
- United States Air Force (USAF) - Crime Prevention Instructor - 1989-1992
- United States Air Force (USAF) - CPR Instructor - 1989-1992
- Federal Emergency Management Agency (FEMA) - Disaster Preparedness Training - 1987-1994

- Green Hill Academy (GH) - Professional Real Estate Career Training on New Home Sales - 1994

- House Hunters (HH) - Sales and Marketing Training - 1997 and 1998

- Champions School of Real Estate (CSRE) - 12 courses across all areas of real estate - 2018

- 75+ classes and courses in the real estate industry over the past three decades

12.6. Community service

- Blood Donor - American Red Cross - Giving blood yearly since 1987

- Self-Aid/Buddy Care Instructor - American Red Cross - Charitably giving my time since 1990

- Goodwill Industries of Central Texas - Charitable giving since 1992

- Poverty Alleviation - The Salvation Army - Charitable giving since 1992

- Canine Companions for Independence - Charitable giving since 1993

- Animal Welfare - Texas Department of Public Safety - Charitable giving since 1994

- Social Services - American Red Cross - Charitable giving since 1994

- Poverty Alleviation - Capital Area Food Bank of Texas - Charitable giving since 1995

- Health Services - American Cancer Society - Charitable giving since 1995

- Proud Texas Native and The Woodlands resident since 1982

- Active volunteer to several community outreach programs since 1985

- Active member of The (WC) Woodlands Church since 1993

- United States Air Force decorated military war veteran, Desert Shield/Desert Storm - 1989-1991

- Multimillion-dollar producer since 1992

- Real estate assistant from 1990 to 1995

- Real estate investor since 1992

- Real estate luxury home sales expert since 1995

- Real estate top producer sales agent since 1998

- Real estate top listing agent since 1998

12.7. Associations and memberships

- National Association of Realtors (NAR)

- Texas Association of Realtors (TAR)

- Houston Association of Realtors (HAR)

- The Woodlands Chamber of Commerce (COC)

- Better Business Bureau (BBB)

- American Business Men's Association (ABMA)

- Air Force Association (AFA)

Chapter 13

Testimonials

— Tom and Kim, Tomball, TX

"We were first-time home buyers and had no idea of the steps to take in purchasing our first home. Every step was explained by Mr. Vaughn R. Shelton ahead of time. Mr. Shelton was there when we looked at our first property and continues to be there for us a month after we've moved into our new home."

— George and Doris, The Woodlands, TX

"Vaughn Shelton, I want to thank you for your outstanding work and salesmanship in the sale of my home. Your professionalism showed through, right from the beginning. I would always feel comfortable referring you."

— Joseph, Conroe, TX

"Working with Mr. Vaughn R. Shelton was a pleasure. By promptly returning phone calls and emails, he made the home-buying experience quite simple for me. He kept me informed every step of the way from searching listings to making an offer on my new home. I highly recommend Vaughn for your next real estate transaction."

— Laurie Burk, The Woodlands, TX

"Thank you for your help and suggestions, which greatly sped up the process of selling our home. We can't believe it sold in less than a week! We would highly recommend your services to anyone moving. You acted in a highly professional and informative manner and it was great getting to know you."

— Chuck Hill, The Woodlands, TX

"Selecting a real estate professional to represent me in the sale of my home was a major decision. After 30 years of mortgage payments and home improvements, I was looking for a professional who could help me realize the best possible return on my investment. Vaughn R. Shelton was the right choice.

— David & Lisa, The Woodlands, TX Vaughn listened closely to my needs, developed a plan with his team specific to my home, and then implemented the plan. It required that we invest in certain improvements and that we follow the recommendations of his team, but it was all worth it. After seven days on the market, Vaughn presented three offers at and above the asking price."

— Marlo Williams, The Woodlands, TX

"If you are looking for a real estate agent, Vaughn R. Shelton, AKA - The Negotiator, is the right real estate agent for you. He sold my house in four days, getting more than we asked. He is extremely professional, personable, and detailed-oriented. He staged my home to sell using a dynamic team consisting of not just him, but a professional stager and photographer as well. His sales results speak for themselves. You will not be disappointed."

— Margaret Smith, The Woodlands, TX

"Mr. Shelton worked with me through the purchase of a new home and the sale of my existing home. He quickly learned what I wanted and found it for me in a few days. He directed me in what I needed to do to sell my existing home and it sold very quickly for very close to my asking price when we listed it."

— Peter, The Woodlands, TX

"Home sale is a daunting ordeal, and Vaughn made it very seamless. For every small detail that came up, Vaughn had an answer or got one at the earliest time he could. I will definitely recommend him to all my friends and family."

— Tom, The Woodlands, TX

"Vaughn R. Shelton is a wonderful person and a wonderful person to work with. He was just awesome throughout the whole process of buying my home. I've already recommended him to someone. Mr. Shelton was just the best of the best!! The home he helped me pick out, me and my family could not be happier!"

— Lynda & Gregg, The Woodlands, TX

"We made the absolute right choice in selecting Vaughn Shelton to sell our home! His personal attention, professionalism, and communication of what buyers expect in our price range were keys in getting our home sold quickly. This has been the best real estate experience we have ever had!"

— David and Joann, The Woodlands, TX

"My experience with Mr. Vaughn R. Shelton was simply outstanding. My wife and I were looking to downsize to a smaller home in a very limited geographical area. He worked with us on a very personal basis and helped us to understand what we really wanted. At one point, Vaughn even told us, 'You might decide to buy this house, but I will not sell it to you!' Vaughn is knowledgeable and always available. He would always show up on short notice and take us to see potential homes. It was his local area knowledge and networking that enabled us to purchase our new home. We simply could not have done this without him. I have been watching the listing since our offer was accepted and there has still not been another home like the one he found!"

— Nancy and Timothy, The Woodlands, TX

"Our home buying experiences with Mr. Shelton began a few years ago with the sale and purchase of a home. All went very smoothly and Vaughn's knowledge base of the area, diligence, and attention to detail made those transactions worry-free. Fast forward a few years, Vaughn again was our first choice to get us into the house of our dreams and to sell our home once again. Vaughn was somehow able to always be one step ahead and ultimately see us through another sale and purchase. When the process seemed daunting, Vaughn was the eternal optimist and reassured us that everything would work out. He also sold our home within hours of listing. From market analysis, contract negotiations, and doing literally whatever it took to get both deals done, Mr. Vaughn R. Shelton was outstanding in terms of his ability to make it happen!! We felt like family and like we were his only client. Highly recommend this agent and friend for your next real estate transaction. He is truly the BEST realtor in Montgomery County!!!"

— **Steve Thompson, Tomball, TX**

"Vaughn was the third realtor that I interviewed to sell my late father's house. My father was an architect and engineer, and had designed the house, which was the home I grew up in. As I showed Vaughn the house, I began to realize that there was something different about him. His questions and comments revealed considerable attention to detail and also knowledge of materials and construction. More importantly, he listened very closely to the story of my father and the house, and therefore could relate to what I was going through on a personal level and understand what I wanted for the property's future. Choosing Mr. Vaughn R. Shelton was the best decision I could have made. His marketing strategy was excellent - he hired a home staging consultant who provided many useful recommendations and a professional photographer who came up with beautiful pictures. The team and Mr. Shelton had an open house that attracted a record attendance, and we received multiple offers, all but one of which was above asking price. Needless to say, the entire experience and the final sale exceeded my expectations."

— Bob Evans, Conroe, TX

"Thank you, Vaughn R. Shelton, for providing me with your wealth of knowledge in putting together a go-to-market strategy and selling the house in just two days! I couldn't have asked for anything more! You provided me with all the right recommendations, starting with help in removing the house from a flood zone to making all optimal enhancements to the property that brought the best possible price that I was hoping for. Your commitment to quality and timeliness in action has really paid off. It was an important step for me to move on to other things in my life!!! Thank you again and I wish you the best!!"

— Michael and Kristin, Lake Conroe, TX

"After several efforts in trying to sell our home, we were a bit disheartened and not sure what direction to take. The house is an amazing, unique property with many perks, it didn't make sense. Neighbors strongly recommended Vaughn Shelton. They espoused his honesty and integrity. On they went, saying he really knows his marketplace and will represent the home on a professional level. As it turned out, that was an understatement. Vaughn is not only professional, but hardworking and willing to make the upfront investment to come onto the market with a splash. He knows how to stage and represent a home. Vaughn also is very respectful of the effort it takes on the part of a homeowner. He takes the time to thoroughly qualify any prospective buyer to assure the match. Wow... what a phenomenal way to go. 9 days, multiple offers. Great advice, great results. Thank you, Vaughn Shelton."

— Pam and Gerald, Tomball, TX

"Vaughn Shelton, you are a true professional. This entire experience can be so overwhelming, and you walked us through every step of the way from selling our home to believing in us, our vision for a new home, and all the business details in between. Your expertise in this field is outstanding, and your patience is commendable. Thank you, Mr. Shelton. It was our pleasure working with you. You were always there for us."

— Brad & Catherine, Houston, TX

"Vaughn Shelton was marvelous. Every detail is taken care of professionally and completely. He is masterful in knowing how to make a house look its best. We feel his use of a home staging consultant and professional photographer really made a difference in the quickness and price of our sale. He is also

personable and wonderful to work with. We would definitely work with him again."

— Tom and Joann, Conroe, TX

"We had the pleasure of working with Vaughn R. Shelton for the sale of our previous home and the purchase of our existing home. It is a challenge to be concise in describing all that Vaughn has done for our family. Mr. Shelton has the unique ability to make us feel as if we are his only client. He is a true professional who cares very much for the clients he serves and delivers on everything he commits to. We recommend Mr. Shelton to anyone buying or selling a home!"

— Steve, Houston, TX

"Mr. Shelton gets it. This is a career for him, not a job. He focuses on continuing education, learning current market trends, house staging, and everything else involved with real estate. As a self-employed person, I spend countless hours learning my craft and just trying to be the best at what I do. I believe it is the best way, long term, to have a successful career. Mr. Shelton does the same, which is why I can appreciate his business. I've encountered many other agents so involved with advertising and recognition that they ignore the fact that being the best at what you do is the most effective advertising. My father and I have a real estate investment business, and it is safe to say Mr. Shelton is a vital part of why we are successful at finding the right homes. Highly recommended; Vaughn Shelton is a true professional."

— **Kimberly, Houston, TX**

"I had a wonderful experience purchasing my new home in Houston. You were so attentive to my needs, very patient, and always available when I had a question. I would definitely recommend you to anyone in the future looking to buy a home."

— Don & Kim, Houston, TX

"Working with you during the process of selling our home was an upbeat, highly professional experience. We were amazed at how quickly the sale happened, and at our asking price, which was right on target with the market research you presented. The attention to detail and added touches you suggested added to the successful sale."

— Joanne, Champions/1960 area, Houston, TX

"Thank you, thank you, thank you, for the warm, personal, and professional manner in which you handled the sale of our home in just 10 days! You were always available to take my calls and handled all questions to ease my fears. Great job to you and the great team you work with."

— John & Liz, Houston, TX

"Thank you so much for helping us find the perfect house. You were so helpful and patient every step of the way. We love it here and will be happy for years."

— Jack & Harriet, Lake Conroe, TX

"Just to let you know how much we appreciate your handling of the sale of our house: We've heard a lot of horror stories about problems arising during real estate transactions. However, your efficient coordinating of our sale was timely and went off without a hitch. We sat back and let you do all the worrying for us. Your professional approach to our sale made things go well. We were new to the use of home staging; however, you made believers of us. We would not hesitate to recommend you to anyone."

— Walter, Tomball, TX

"Thank you for your professional efforts in selling my house. You have given added meaning to organization, timeliness, and flexibility. Your style and process should be a benchmark for a lot of other realtors. You are easy to work with and alongside."

— Amy & James, Conroe, TX

"Vaughn, we really do appreciate your follow-through. You have made the closing process stress-free for us. Your customer service is just impeccable

& we would highly recommend you to anyone who is thinking about selling their home."

— Anthony & Deborah, The Woodlands, TX

"Thank you again for the tremendous job you did in finding us a house and making sure it closed as scheduled. The circumstances were very difficult, and we greatly appreciate your tenacity in dealing with the sellers."

— William & Maryanne, Houston, TX

"Thank you so very much for all the hard work put into helping us acquire our home. Your professionalism throughout and your attention to all details were outstanding. It was a sincere pleasure doing business with you."

— Joseph, Carol & Susan, Conroe, TX

"Thank you so much for all your hard work in getting our mother's home sold so quickly.

Dear Homeowner,

I noticed that you have placed your home on the market and that your listing expired without a successful sale or you are still trying to sell the home with no sale.

As a realtor, I am very familiar with your area. I have completed many successful sales near your home and feel certain that I can help you accomplish your goals regarding the sale of your property.

Of course, we all know that a successful sale requires a successful plan. I have a well-established base in your area, and I am prepared to sit down with you and share some things your previous agent may have missed.

Selling your home is one of the most important financial decisions you can make. Normally, one's home is their most valuable asset. There are key ingredients in devising a marketing strategy that will help ensure that you receive the full financial potential available to you through the sale of your home. In addition, that same well-planned strategy can minimize the amount of time your home is on the market. The first key ingredient is to select the right realtor.

I would love the opportunity to sit down with you to present a marketing plan that I know will produce great results for you. Please contact me on my cell phone number at 281-221-4676 or email me at vaughn@vaughnshelton.com or vaughnrshelton@gmail.com.

Having viewed your property's previous listing and your property, I am certain that you will be satisfied with the outcome of our meeting.

Sincerely,

Vaughn Ray Shelton, Jr.

"World Class Experience = World Class Service"